MY HAUNTED BASEMENT

A Mystery By

RYKEE BELL

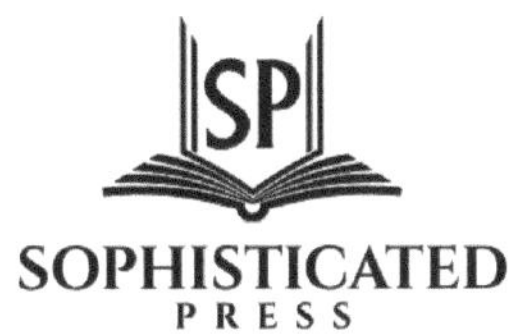

SOPHISTICATED PRESS

Printed in the United States of America

Publisher: Sophisticated Press
Illustrator: Rykee Bell

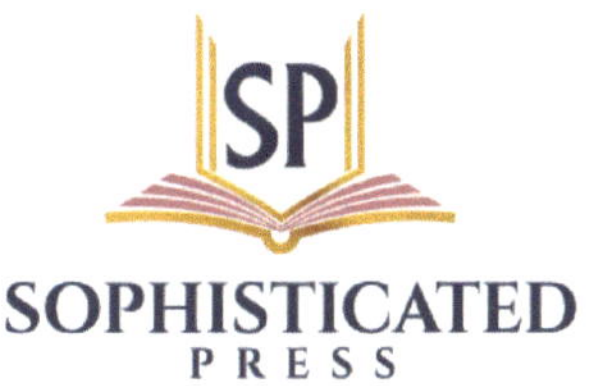

DEDICATION

Dedicated to Patice D. Thompson for being a phenomenal parent with unwavering support.

Thank you to Sophisticated Sentences for investing in voices of the future through their literary writing program.

TABLE OF CONTENTS

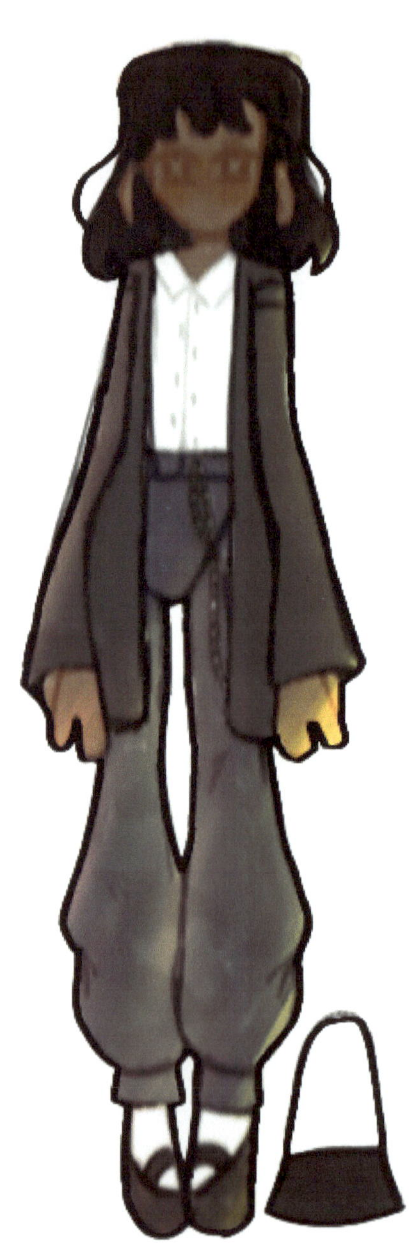

THE BORED

It was a cloudy Wednesday with nothing to do. Today, I have decided just to stay home and do nothing because there is nothing to do besides just playing on my phone for hours on end, as you can see how bored I am. My name is Rykee, and I'm 13 years old. It's now summer break, and it has got to be the most boring summer ever because every day, all I do is sleep all day and stay up all night, so to pass the time, I just started counting down the days until school starts back.

As I started to toss and turn in my bed finally, I fell asleep and had a strange dream. I see a hand, blood, my family, and me being in shock and scared, then I look over and see the words DEAD.

I woke up in a cold sweat because of the dream, but I decided not to question it because people always have weird dreams. This was just one of them.

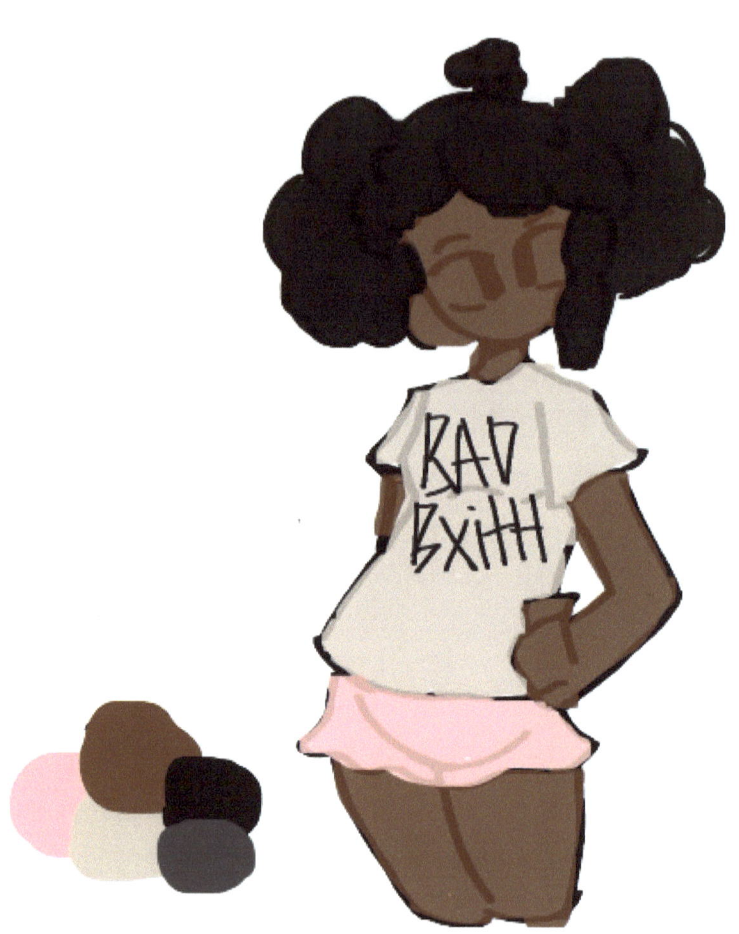
RAD
BXiHH

I slowly got up from my bed, and strangely, I looked at my phone; it said Thursday at 7 a.m. Mom should be up getting ready to go to work. I walk up to her room quietly to see if she is up. There she was, looking at her phone, chuckling. She asked me to go see if my brother was ready.

I go downstairs to see if my brother is awake and see some weird patterns on the floor. I didn't pay any attention because I was rushing to my brother's room to wake him up, but I didn't see anyone in his room, and then I heard yelling from outside. They kept saying my kids were missing. But here's where my Summer just got interesting.

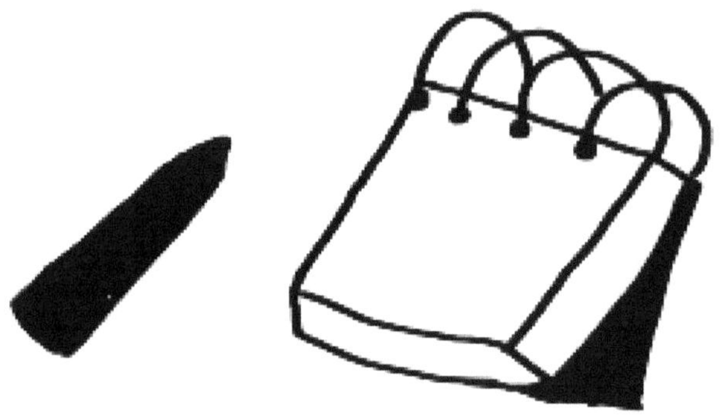

THE INVESTIGATION BEGINS

As I rushed up the stairs in a hurry to tell my mom that Jalen wasn't there, I almost tripped up the stairs.

Entering my mother's room immediately in a flash, I say, "Jalen is not there." I think he's missing. I checked, and he's not there." I pleaded with my mom. She responded, "I swear to God, if you're playing with me, I will be mad at you." She heads down the stairs. A few moments later, she says, " Are you sure you didn't see him?" Quickly, I responded, "No," as Mom went to call 911 again. I decided to check out the people in our neighborhood. As I stepped out of the house with a journal and a pen. I searched for somebody to interview since I couldn't think of anyone at the moment. I took a sit on the chair that was on the porch. I sat down with my legs crossed with my journal in my lap.

I write down the victim's names on the page and look up to find someone who looks the most distressed and worried. I decided to interview Johnny Lee, Kate Winston, and Anastasia Quinn. Johnny Lee was first because he seemed the most distressed out of the three. As I walk up to his house, I see him crying on the porch, covered with a towel. He looked like he could break any second. As I approached the porch, I asked, "Hey, Mr. Johnny, may I talk to you about what happened?" Waving me off, Johnny responds, "Maybe another time, Rykee? I'm not in the mood right now." I nodded, went back down the stairs, and decided to come back later to try again.

As I pondered which one to go to next, I decided to go to Anastasia Quinn's house. I talked to her for a while with questions. All I got from her was that she didn't know how her son was gone because she got a message from him that he would be home at 2 a.m. or 3 a.m.

Then I went over to Kate Winston's house, and she told me a similar story that took an hour. Before going to Johnny's house, I waited 30 minutes.

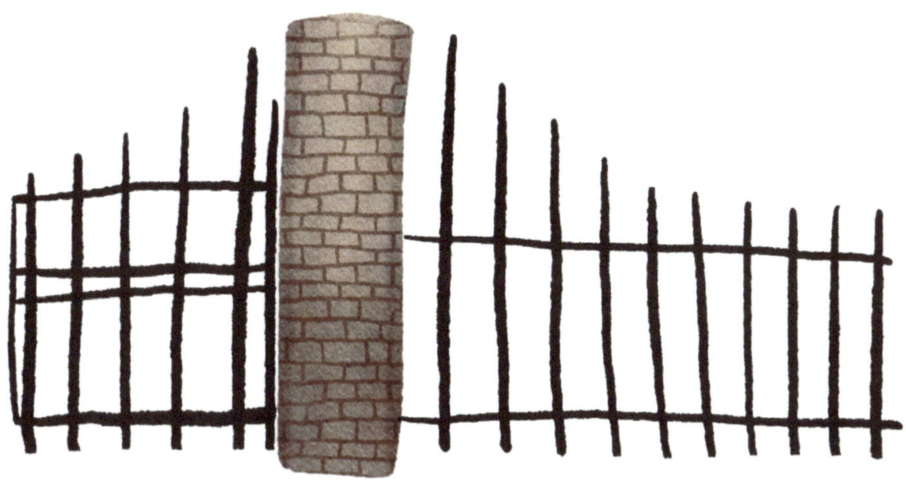

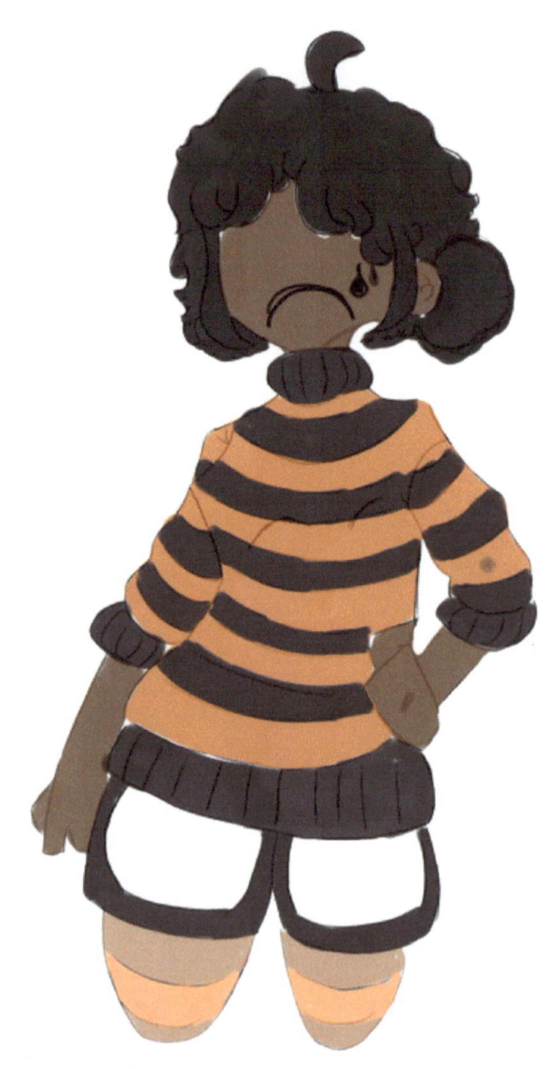

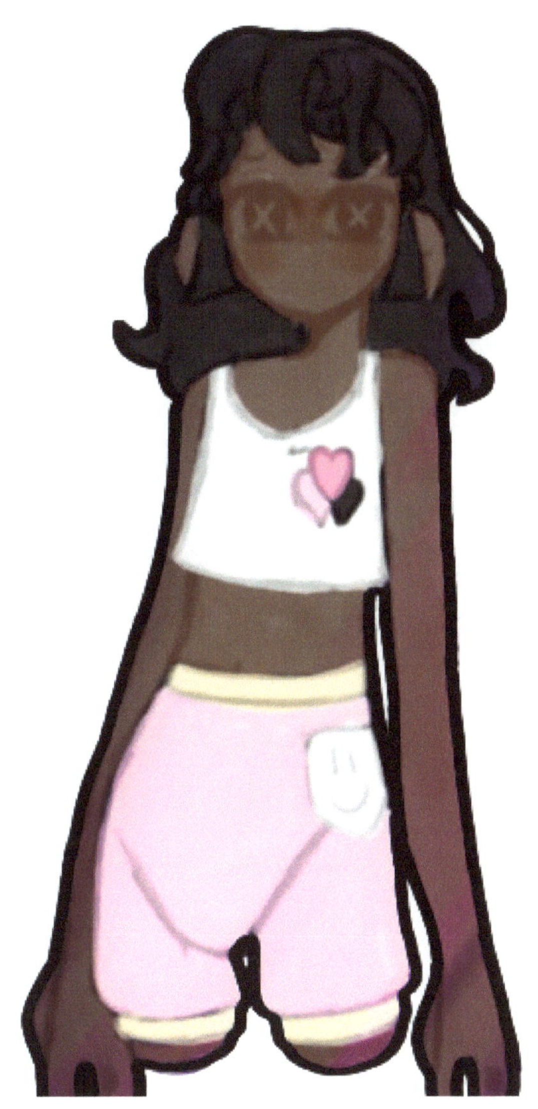

THE DETECTIVE & THE KILLER

As I started to head over to Johnny's house again, I found him writing a letter in a journal. He seemed serious about it as well. I went over and said, "What are you writing over there, John?" " I don't want to talk about it," John said.

Okay, that was unexpected. He usually tells me everything, no matter what, whether it is his money, his kids, or his wife. He would have told me. I don't know why he likes me the most. "Are you ready to answer my questions now?" I inquired. "Yeah, just give me a moment," John responded. Sitting back in my chair and looking around, I was happy it only took a minute. He raised his head and looked at me. He looked tired, scared, lost, and afraid. At the same time, he spoke in a low tone as he started to tell me his story: "It was a normal morning, just like today for most people. I was looking for my wife and two kids.

I noticed that they were gone, so I went to look for them. I went to the kitchen, where I found…" His voice went quiet for a moment as he tried to collect himself.

 "I saw blood on the floor," and he started to get emotional. "My older son is on the floor with his arm gone and blood on his face. He looks like he is torn apart." I stand up and hug him while rubbing his back. "Take a moment," I insist. "Okay, I'm fine now. I can continue. Now he is gone from this world, gone from me. I ran to him, terrified. I didn't know what to do. All I could do was stare at him with his blood on my hands now, and then I was thinking, how can someone do this? It's inhumane, and why not me?"

He goes silent, and then, at that next moment, he continues.

"I remember the night before he said he was going in the basement with his brother."

I head down the stairs to hear munching. I questioned myself about it. I still didn't know where it came from, but it was close, and I think it was eating. Don't say it if you don't understand. Okay? I see my younger son with his eyes bucked out of his skull and both of his arms gone. It was horrific."

He is now crying, and I guess his wife heard the screams and came down, and her head is gone. He breakdowns crying hysterically.

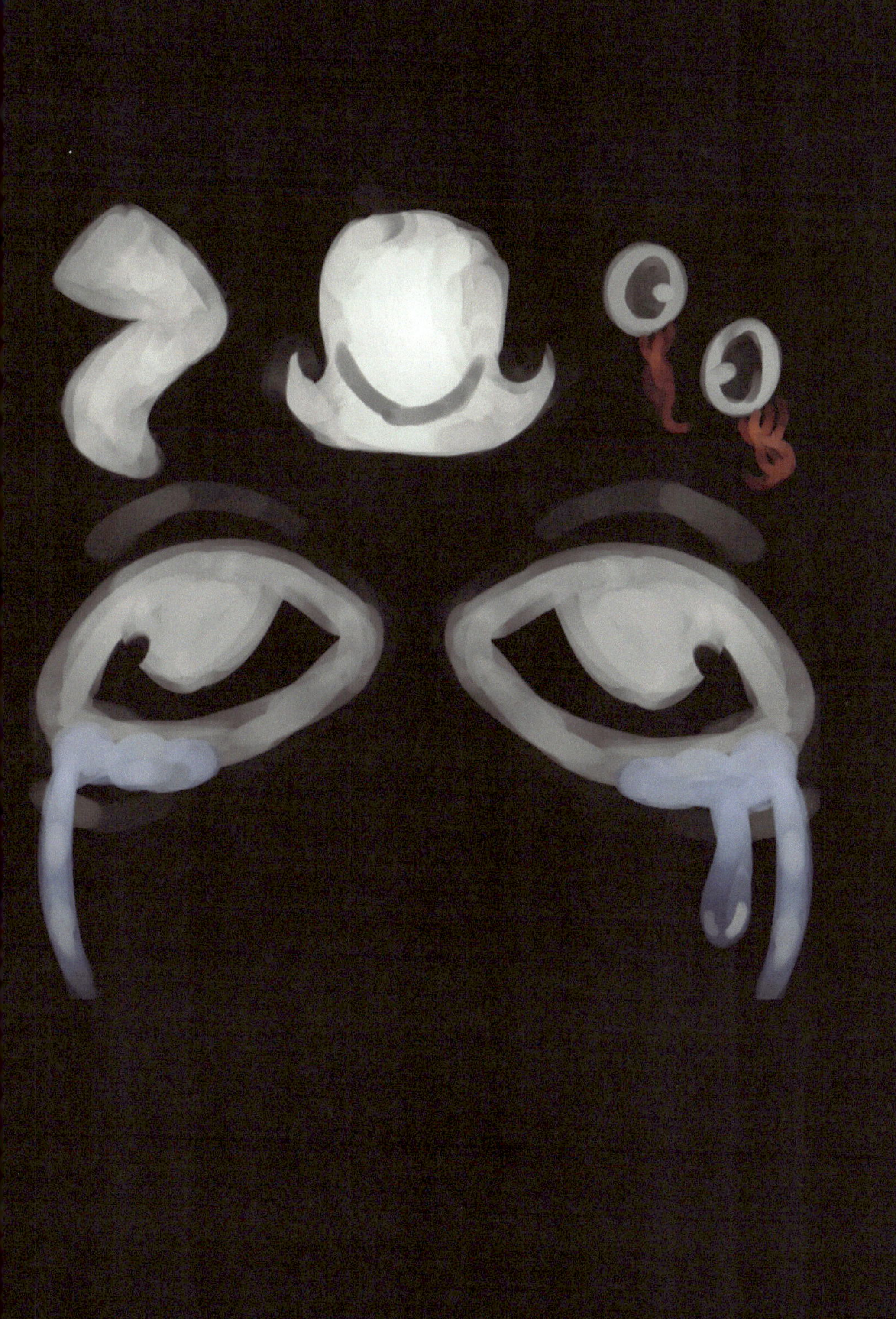

THE DARK WEB

I rushed to hug him because he had just found out that his whole family was dead; I would be in an unconsolable state as well if I were in his situation. It took an hour and 30 minutes to calm down, and after that, I said my farewells and left.

But before that, I gave him my contact information so he could call me and give me more details when he was ready.

I started to head home and saw the police start to leave our house. They gave Mom a warning, which I couldn't make out. The Officer said, " Stay home." as he headed into his car. I walk up to my mother to see what's happening. She said, "The police told us to stay home for a week or two and that they got the situation under control." She walks back into the house, looking worried and scared but also angry. I can tell that she doesn't think they do.

I head up the stairs to tell her what I heard from the people in the other neighborhood. I take one last glance at John and go up the stairs to my house again. When we went inside, my mom got on the couch and asked me, "Okay, what did they say in a low tone?" As I started to talk in the cold, aired room, I reflected that the people I talked to had one thing in common: it had to be something about their kids going missing, like my brother. Mom nodded, but that one was a little different. This had to do with a murder. I looked at my mom, who only had a blank stare on her face to match the cold room perfectly.

I begin to share, "I went over to Johnny Lee's place, and he looked scared, horrified, and emotionless, and he told me that his whole family had died. He also shared that it looked horrible. His kids were missing their eyes, legs, and arms, and his wife was missing her whole head." As I motioned for my mom to look at me now. She was full of worry and asked, "Is he going to be all right? "No," I replied.

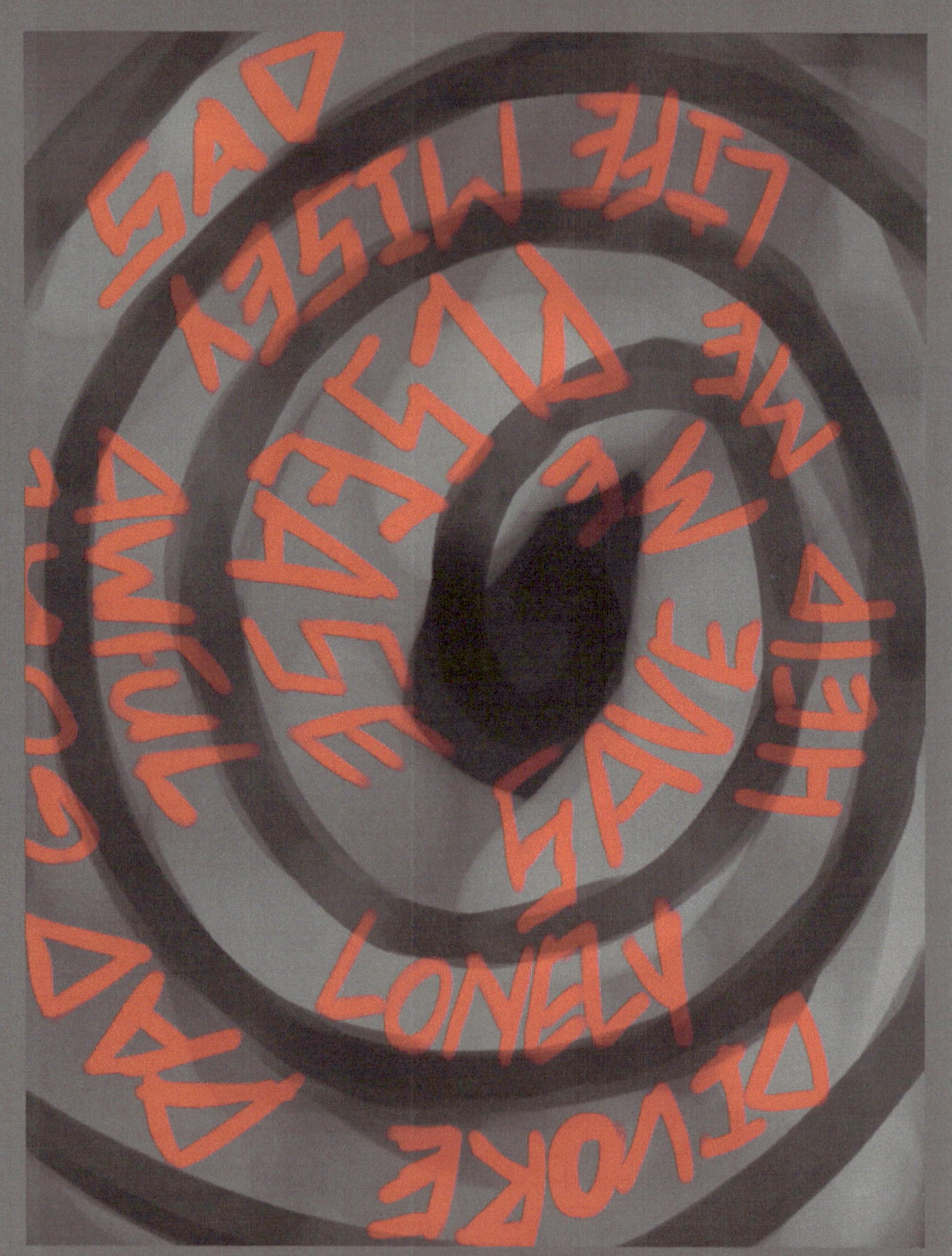

SAD
LIFE MISERY
MISERY
AWFUL
MISERY
ME
HELP
SAVE
LONELY
DIVORCE
BAD

THE RESEARCH OF THE NIGHT

I started to walk to my room to get change. My mom grabbed my arm with fear in her eyes and told me, "Hey, whatever you're going to do, don't do it. You know investigating gets you killed."

"I will be fine," I said as I entered my room to get changed. I looked outside to see if my mom was still there, and she wasn't. I quickly hurried to my laptop and typed up the missing cases, which took two minutes. I scrolled to see that there were a lot of missing cases. In total, it was 22,960 cases worldwide.

There are also murder cases as well today. There were also pictures of the murders, and they were gruesome and inhumane. It was the same thing as Johnny described. As I scrolled down some more to see more lifeless dead faces, tears of sorrow and misery began to fall on my cheeks. I returned to the search bar and typed up the missing case on March 1, 2022.

I hit search to see a dozen names, such as Alice Goodman, Jake Goodwill, Marcy Belle, etc. Since I wanted to talk to people on my street, I went back to the search bar to search for missing cases near me and saw that there were. To my surprise, I saw all the people in my neighborhood. I started to scroll to see who to interview. I looked at all the names on the tread, and two names caught my attention: Miss Abigail and Lee Martin. These two used to be together until Miss Abigail had an affair with a rich man that is 50 years old and had a divorce a year ago, and his wife took the kids.

 Abigail had two kids with Lee: Sasha, who is 6, and Carly, who is 9. I don't talk to them often, but they were good kids by heart. They both got straight As and were perfect at everything, but after their parents got a divorce, they started to fail in school.

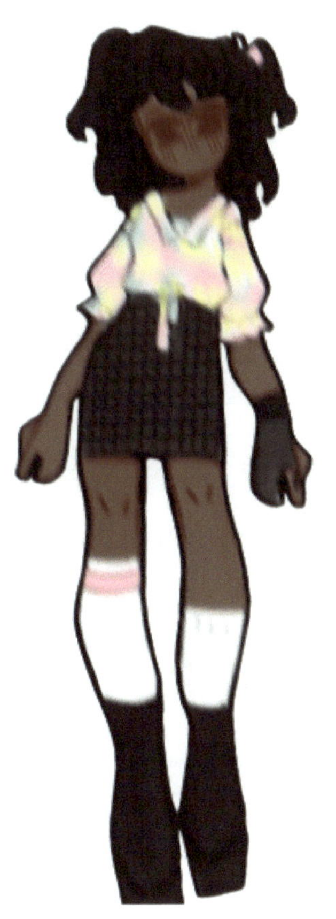

THE LIES FILLED WITHIN

I decided to do it tomorrow because it's now 2 a.m., and everyone's probably asleep. I got up out of my chair and changed into my pajamas. I flopped on my bed and got under my blanket. Everything felt so warm, like I was at the beach, and my hands felt warm. It was so peaceful.

Until I heard a noise, I knew that if I investigated this, I would get killed also. I decided to stay still, close my eyes, and breathe slowly until I fell asleep. I woke up in t at 3:30 a.m. I struggled to get out of the warmth of my blanket, and as soon as I did, I saw my mom in her room looking miserable. I walked up to her with a sigh. "Hey, are you all right?" as I leaned on her bedside.

"Well, you know I'm just worried about Jalen. That's all I know. It's going to be all right." I say as I pat her on her back in sorrow. It's going to be okay I said as I whispered this was the first time I cared about my brother.

At that moment, I felt worried and fearful for my brother, whom I had hated ever since I was little. Sure, I hated him, but he was still my brother, and I loved him more. It was just sibling rivalry, and I wanted him to come home so Mom would stop being stressed. I was worried sick so that we could make sure he was okay and safe. I hugged her tight, let her go, patted her on the back again, and told her I would be going out again to investigate more. I took a shower, washed my face, brushed my teeth, and got dressed into something more classy and modern for the day's activities. I headed out of the house to prepare for a long walk because the houses were miles away.

I decided to walk there and take a shortcut, which would be a 30-minute walk. While I was walking, I noticed the pretty trees, leaves, flowers, and bushes. Then I suddenly remembered something in my pocket that I needed to check because I didn't want to die or get kidnapped.

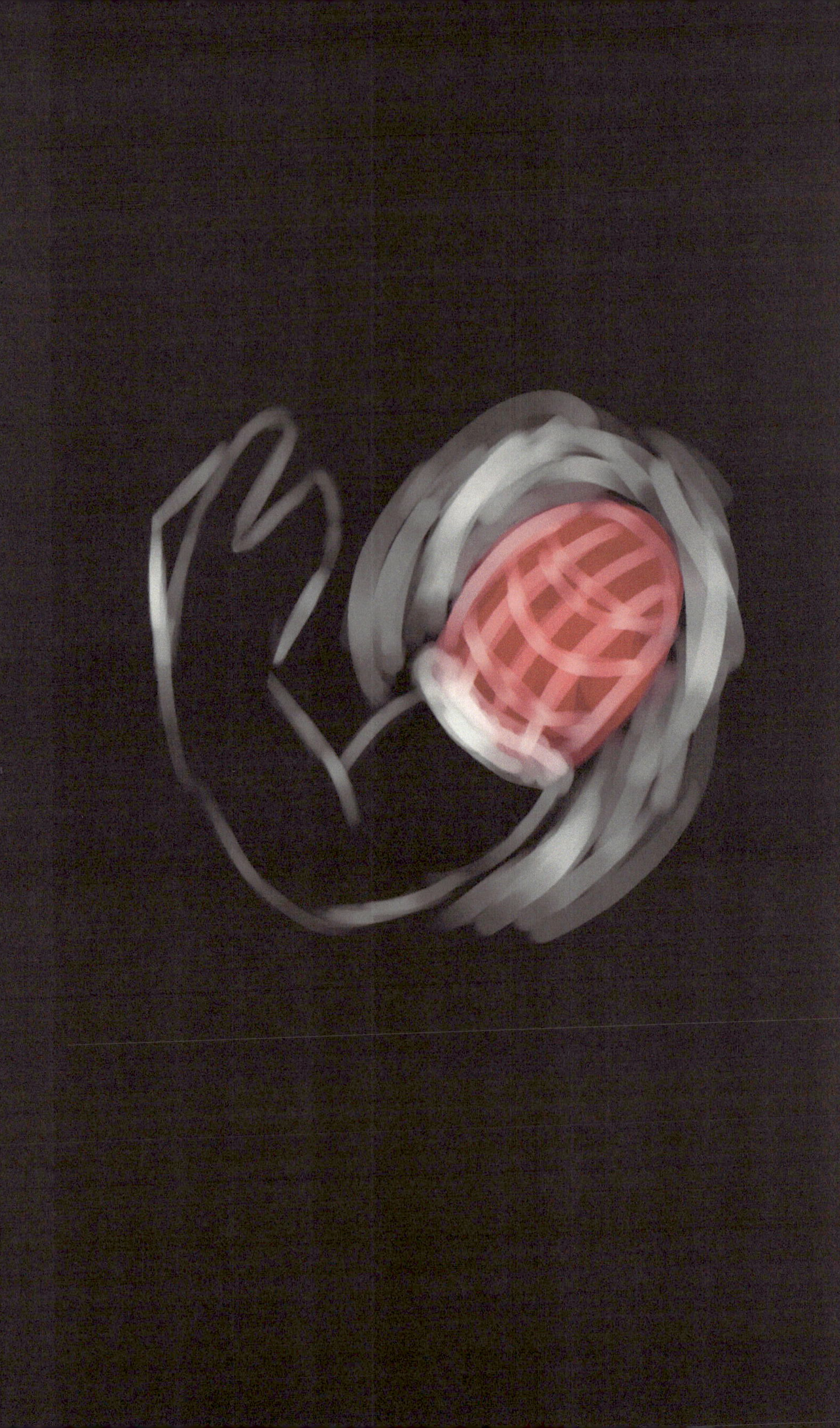

The 5 Day Stay

After walking for about 30 minutes, I reached Lee's house. It looked empty and soulless like no one had lived there in years. I decided to ignore it and I walked up to his door, feeling an eerie chill up my spine.

I gently knocked on his door and said hello. I did it again, then I tapped a little bit louder then decided to give up. I went to the window of the house to see that it was pretty empty and that it was collecting dust with spider webs. I went to the next-door neighbor's house to see if they saw the Lee's. I knocked on the door, gently dusted off my shoulders, and waited for someone to answer. I did it again, and then, finally, someone answered. It was a middle-aged woman looking annoyed at me, and I said I don't want any of your Girl Scout cookies. Ok, um, no, I'm not here to sell any Girl Scout cookies, ma'am.

Then she said what are you here for? I just wanted to know what happened to that house over there. I said as I pointed to the house next door. I said that old thing over there. The man over there moved out about a month ago. Oh, I said, that's why the house is so dead inside, huh? She said yep.

Well, I will be on my way. Bye, I said as I was leaving the house. I heard the door slam behind me. I decided to interview Abigale, but I remembered that she was with the kids on vacation.

I started to walk back to my house, but something caught my eye. It was an alley and a creepy one at that. There was a big and a large hand coming from it. The hand looked like it belonged to a builder, so I ignored it and kept walking. It had been five days.

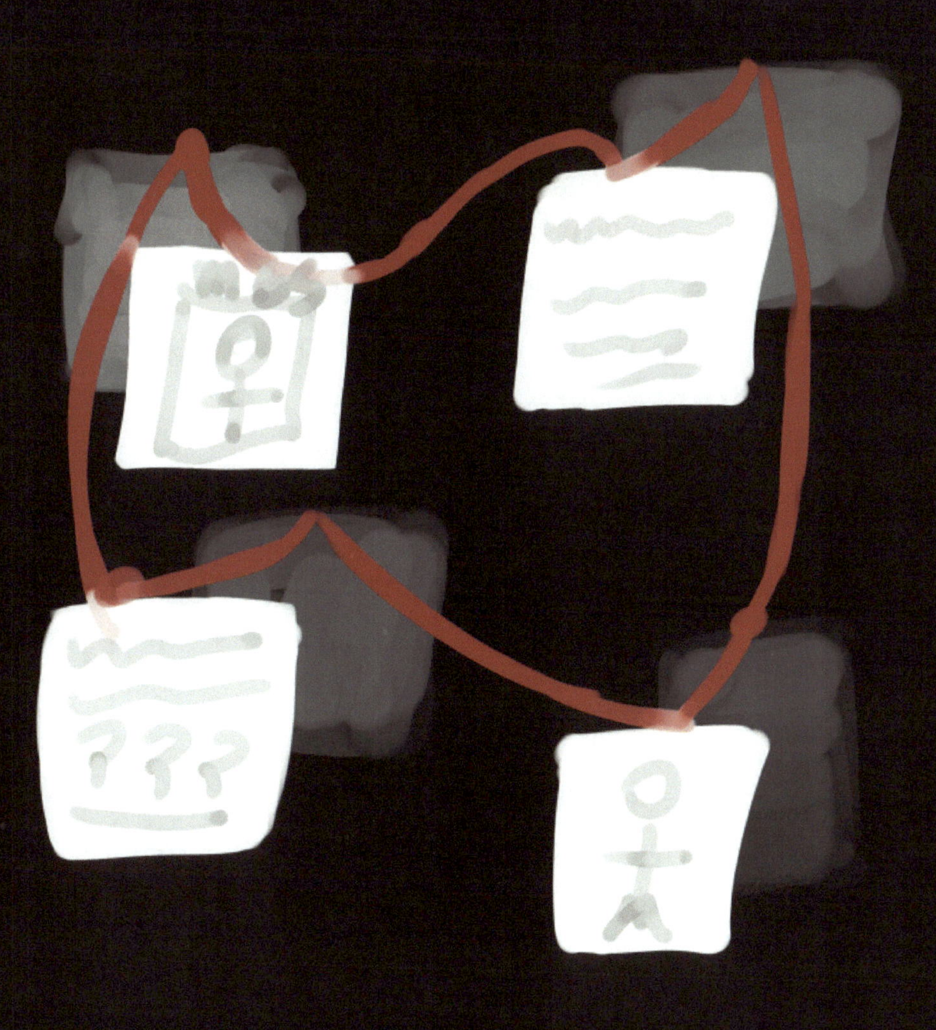

THE RETURN OF THE DEAD

It was 5 days since my little brother was missing. I learned some new information about the missing cases. I have learned five more things in these cases: that all the kids were already or on their way home and that all the parents were asleep then.

And the strangest thing of all is that every single one of them is connected to the basements. I looked down at the notepad on which I had written all my information and looked up in confusion. While I was in thought, I heard a knock on the door, then my mother's footsteps walked up to the door, and then there was dead silence and tears. I walked carefully to see my mom at the door with her hands together close like she was praying I move forward trying not to think of the worse.

I saw my brother with a big, goofy smile on his face about to hug my mom. They smiled and hugged tightly, rocking back and forth. Then they saw me, and I joined in. I was so happy to have my family back together. I didn't want this feeling to end; I just wanted to stand there and take it all in.

We all let out with the happiest of tears. Mom hit his arm and said where have you been? We were worried sick about you looking angry. Then he said I was at Jay's house. Remember I told you she was like, no, you didn't. He said yes, I told you I would be back on Thursday, but I lost track of time and came home late.

Oh well, I guess I didn't get that message. At least we know that you are safe and not hurt. Then my mom went quiet for a moment until Jalen said well, I'm going to go to the basement. Just call me if you need me. All is well, so I go flop on the couch, looking relieved and happy that we are all together again in peace until a horrible scream comes.

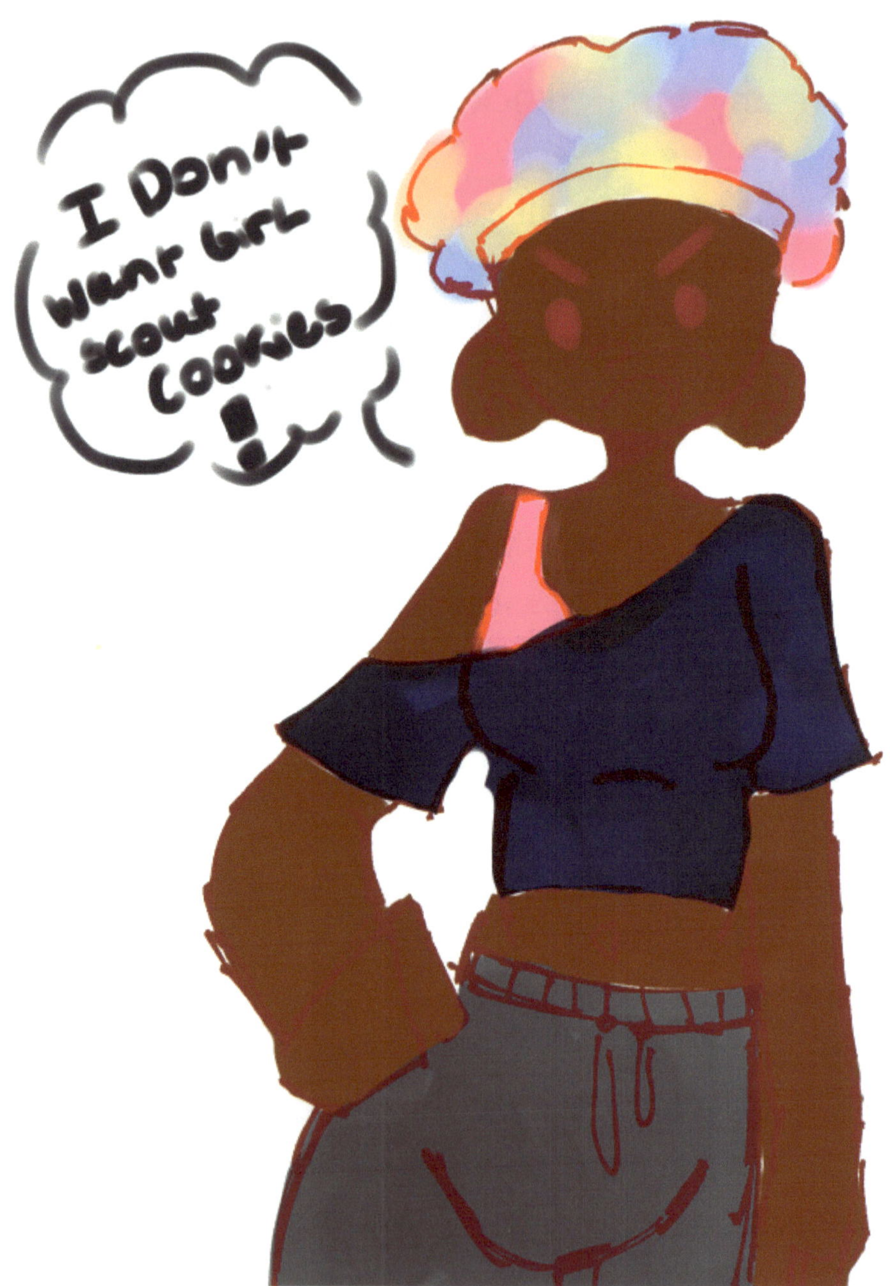

I Don't
Want GirL
scout
cookies
!

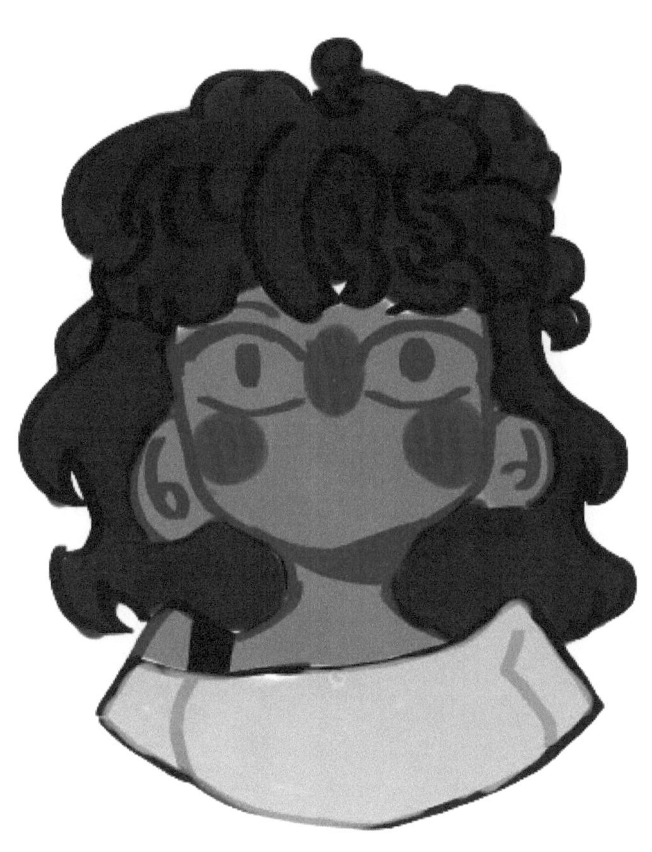

THE WHITE VOID OF NOTHING

I rushed down the stairs to see my brother pitifully banging on a large hand that I had seen before, the one in the alley with the blood on him and the hand coming through the shadows of the basement.

I slowed down to get a closer look at what was happening right now. I was stunned to see that same hand move up to the ceiling, and a mouth appeared. I was unable to move when the mouth was eating our cat Joy, and all the screams and shouts blurred my vision. Everything in my mind was going crazy as the muffled cries and screeching continued. I was confused. What could I do to reverse this? I meant to be alone forever. Did I not deserve happiness? I just didn't understand why, but then I looked up, scared to see the monster itself in front of me with Joy's blood on it.

Looking at me with a big toothy grin, I looked at it scared, heart beating hard and fast enough to hear for miles. I started to feel light-headed, and the last thing I heard was run !!!

I woke up in a place in a white void, all alone. There was nothing but pure white. I struggled to get up and rubbed the temple of my head to remove the dizziness and pressure from my head.

As I searched for a way to get out and find safety, after about 30 to 40 minutes of walking around, I realized I was probably just getting myself lost, so I sat on my knees and cried because I was alone and scared and just wanted to go home to my family. Then, someone tapped me on my shoulder. It..................

To be continued

ABOUT THE AUTHOR

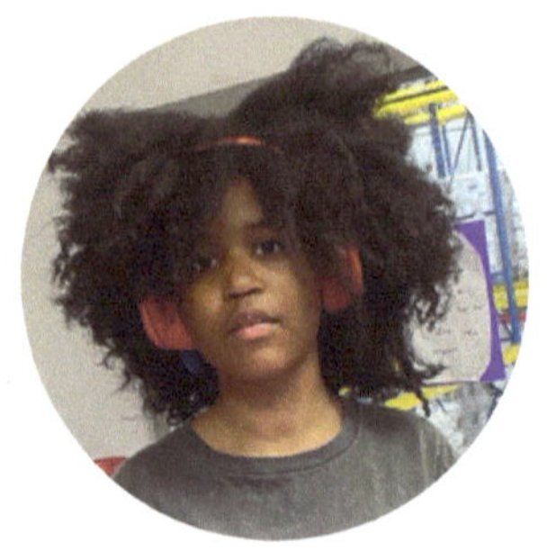

Rykee Bell is a shy, fun, and loving creative. She loves art, and she has been self-taught since the age of 5. My Haunted Basement is her first Illustrated book created by her own pen!

She loves mysteries, gaming, and drawing. Join Rykee in exploring her haunted basement and help her solve the mystery. This is book one of a mini-series written by Rykee Bell.

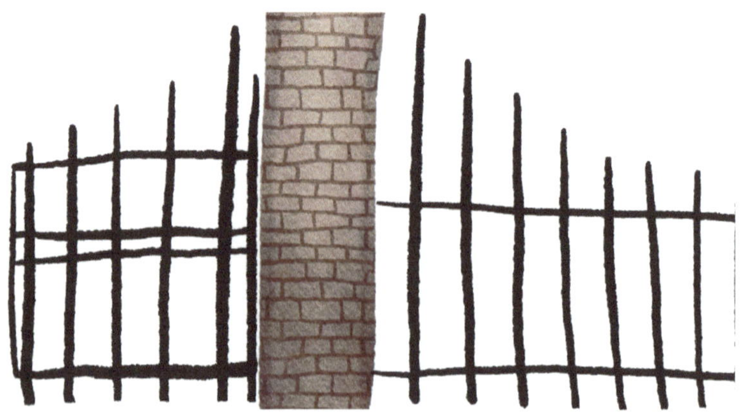